Diving Back In

~*A Guide to Getting the Most Out of Swimming*~

Max Charles Munson

Copyright © 2021 Max Charles Munson

All rights reserved. No part of this book may be reproduced, stored, or transmitted by any means—whether auditory, graphic, mechanical, or electronic—without written permission of both publisher and author, except in the case of brief excerpts used in critical articles and reviews. Unauthorized reproduction of any part of this work is illegal and is punishable by law.

Contents

Acknowledgments 4

It Was Just Lunch 5
A Love-Hate Relationship 7
A Competitive Start 10
Becoming an "Adult Swimmer" 16
Thinking Outside the Pool 29
Beyond the Race 37
Getting Started or Re-started 39
The Commitment 41
Diving In 44

Appendix A 56
Appendix B 60

Acknowledgments

I would like to thank my wife for her understanding and encouragement during the writing of this book. She helped to keep me going and to better understand my audience. Thank you, Marcela!

I would also like to thank my father, Lester Munson Jr., and my brother, Lester Munson III, for patiently and enthusiastically helping me with the editing process. Thank you, Pop and Les!

I would also like to thank the Neptun Masters swim team in Prague for its support for my swimming endeavors, and for their dedication to swimming in general.

It Was Just Lunch

The surprise came early in our lunch. Only a few minutes after we sat down at a table in the pub restaurant I owned and operated in the center of Prague, Czech Republic, my friend, a Czech real estate guy, told me he had just returned from the European Masters Swim Championships in London. What? Wait a minute, I thought. Swim competitions for middle-aged guys like us? Over the time we had known each other, I knew he was athletic, had been involved in basketball and volleyball leagues. But this was something new.

Right away, to my amazement, I found myself interested. From age 8 to my freshman year in college, I had competed in age-group swimming. I had trained 11 months of the year with two practices each day; I had piled up ribbons and trophies; and I had given it up. I had no idea there was a Masters swim organization, much less an organization on a scale that was staging European championships. I suddenly found myself wondering whether I was ready to get back in the pool after so much time out of the water. Could I become a Masters swimmer? I did not know it at the time, but the answers to these questions changed my life and put me on a path where everything was better.

A Love-Hate Relationship

During my senior year in college, I wrote a paper titled, "Don't Let Your Babies Grow Up to Be Age-Group Swimmers." I was disillusioned with competitive swimming and wanted to convince others to stay away from it. From the ages of 8 to 18 I had been a year-round swimmer (a.k.a age-group), often swimming twice a day to stay in top shape. There was no off-season. All day, every day, I was either on my way to practice, at practice, or returning from practice. Throughout my teens I had the feeling of being perpetually exhausted, often falling asleep during classes in middle school and high school. At 21 years old, almost four years after quitting the sport, I was still resentful that I had "wasted" those important years of my life, squandered them on a sport that nobody in the world seemed to care about, except swimmers themselves.

That was more than 30 years ago, and surprisingly my thinking has now come around full circle. These days I am not only thankful for all those countless hours in the pool, I have gone from being a swim agnostic to a swim evangelist, ready to share with the rest of the world all of the benefits a swimmer receives and enjoys from his or her time in the water.

Let's start by answering the question, what is a "swimmer"? For the purposes of this book, a swimmer is anyone who enjoys getting in the water, whether it be a 50-meter Olympic-sized pool, a recreational pool, an ocean, or a lake, and getting in some distance. How much distance? I would say that starting at about 500 meters per session is a decent minimum. And of course, there is no maximum. If you are getting in the pool and swimming breaststroke for 500m, then as far as I am concerned you can consider yourself a swimmer. If 500m seems like too much, and yet you want to become a swimmer, then that should be your first goal. You can get there with practice and, depending on your stroke, some instruction. Going from short distances at first to around a kilometer per workout is akin to going from duffer to golfer. Once you can swim far enough to get some exercise, to get your mind focused, and to have something to build on, then you are ready to take advantage of all that swimming has to offer.

In the following pages I will explore the various ways that you can maximize the enjoyment of your swimming, not to mention improve it. This is not a how-to book on stroke technique. For that there are recommended books in the appendix. Instead, this book breaks down the ways to maximize the joy and satisfaction that you can get from the water.

A Competitive Start

But first, a bit more on my original ups and downs in the water, and what brought me full circle on swimming in general. What turned me off about swimming, and then prompted that anti-swimming manifesto in college, was the focus on winning. In the United States we are overly concerned with being the best, buying "the best," or seeking out "the best." Winning is a great motivator, as long as you have a chance at the gold. I understand that to go to the top of any sport there must be a certain amount of ego involved, and that winning is the only way up. And for those people who get to the top, or at least approach it, that works. But what about for the rest of us? If the focus is too much on winning, then when we don't win, we are moving down the ladder instead of up. We can lose our motivation very quickly.

It was this misplaced focus that drained much of my interest in swimming. From ages 8 to 14, I improved my times rapidly and moved up to the top meets quickly, often finishing in the top three. As I grew older and moved in to the 15- to 18-year-old category, the field of competition became more competitive, and I found it harder and harder to stay at the top. By the time I was finishing high school I had gone from being a top swimmer in the state of Illinois, to just another swimmer hoping to win my preliminary heat and to make it into the final heat of a big race. I wondered again and again: If I am not finishing at least in the top three, why am I doing this?

My priorities had not always been so skewed. As a kid I had loved the water, swimming in all the local outdoor pools whenever it was warm enough, and in the lake when we would go on summer vacations. If the weather was nice, I wanted to swim. I loved the feeling of diving in, the refreshing coolness, the buoyancy, and the fun. Water equaled fun. We would snorkel through the lake looking for treasures. I would put on fins and fly underwater like Superman. We would float on inner tubes, water ski, chase each other around in the water. I was game to get in any time. As I got older and joined various swim teams, I held lifeguard jobs in high school, and coached a local team my senior year. I enjoyed swimming and wanted to stay close to it. As I got faster, the competitions started getting larger, the training more challenging, and the intensity increased. It wasn't about the fun anymore (or at least rarely so). It was about winning and getting to the next level.

    I then had one experience that really brought to head how done I was with competitive swimming. As I toured universities, I interviewed with the swim team coaches at the University of North Carolina, the University of Southern California, and then at Arizona State University. A couple of the interviews went fine, and although I was not a fast enough swimmer to get offered a scholarship, most teams would have been happy to welcome me as a "walk-on" on their team. But at ASU the meeting did not go well. I met the coach at the side of the pool for our scheduled interview during a practice session. I had been used to tours of the facilities and then interviews with coaches in their offices, but here it was clearly different. He walked me to the end of the pool while occasionally yelling at his swimmers and asked me my times in my various events (the 100m, 200m and 400m freestyle). By the time we returned to the starting end of the pool he shook my hand and said, "I'm sorry, those times just aren't fast enough." He then turned and walked along the pool, barking out commands at his various swimmers. I was devastated. Ten years of swimming, often four hours a day of practice, of countless weekends lost to competitions, and my reward was to be dissed in a 2-minute interview? I was done with competitive swimming and good riddance.

Diving Back In

It was just a few years later that I wrote the "Don't Let Your Babies Grow Up to Be Age-Group Swimmers" paper, hoping to get on the page exactly why kids should not waste their time joining swim teams. I ended up going to ASU, and because I could not make the swim team, I joined the water polo club. (I may have been far from the best water polo player, but at least I could get back and forth quickly.) I never considered swimming again after that interview. Instead, I regretted not playing other sports and developing an ability in the various seasonal sports such as basketball, baseball, and football. I was 6' 4", 220 pounds, and I couldn't shoot a basketball. If someone passed a ball to me, I was not sure I could catch it. Throughout college, when my friends were playing intra-mural games and tournaments, I was on the sideline, not adept enough to compete on their level. I began to resent the fact that my formative years were spent in the pool rather than developing the skills that everyone else seemed to have.

When the focus is on being the best, as I had been doing my entire swimming career, then you are setting yourself up for disappointment. There will always be a faster swimmer. If not now, then later. There will always be pitfalls, illnesses, time constraints, broken bones, or something to prohibit you from being (and staying) the best. For me it was a heavy bout of mononucleosis and shoulder injuries. These things can cause undue amounts of stress as you see your chances of winning diminish with each practice you miss. Yes, sometimes you might bring home the top prize, but then so very often you will not. It was this overemphasis on winning that inhibited me from getting any enjoyment out of swimming unless I was on the podium. So when I wasn't even allowed on the ASU swim team, let alone having a chance at being one of the top swimmers on it, it killed any remaining attachment I still had to the sport. All due to a focus on the wrong priorities.

In swimming (and indeed in many other aspects of life), I needed to adjust my goals and focus on the things that were within my control. I had to learn how to gain pleasure and satisfaction not from victory (although that can be a nice by-product) but from the process itself. "The process" includes it all: the practices, the stretching, the conversations and camaraderie with other swimmers, the weight training, and the competitions. Depending on your level of swimming, it can also include the amount of sleep you get, your eating habits, your yoga practice, even your transportation to and from practices. It was time for me to change my focus from the podium to the process. It was by doing this that I became able to enjoy swimming again.

My transformation from writing that paper to becoming an advocate for swimming all began with a change in priorities. No longer would the focus be on winning, it would be on enjoying as many aspects as possible of the "process." But just being an adult is not enough to automatically appreciate the process. You need to work at it. We are programmed by society, media, social media, coaches, parents, and peers - especially in America - with an overemphasis on being the best, on winning, rather than enjoying the ride. Overcoming this programming is not easy.

Becoming an "Adult Swimmer"

For 30 years I did not compete as a swimmer. Occasionally I would jump in a pool and swim a few laps. But I probably did that only a couple dozen times in total over that period. It did not occur to me than anybody after college still swam in an organized program. I had this preconceived notion that it was the Olympics or nothing. I worked on my career, got married, and raised a family well into my 40s. I was blissfully unaware that people still competed in middle age, not to mention in old age. I would go to the gym or go running or occasionally cycle, but was not part of any organized sport and had not been since water polo in college. It wasn't until that fateful lunch with my friend where, over burgers, he told me about the world of Masters swimming.

Diving Back In

I had never even heard of Masters swimming. Of course, I would watch the "Masters" on TV each year, but that was golf. There were Masters swimmers too? I wanted to know more. He explained that just as there was age-group swimming for kids, there was age-group swimming for adults, and it was called Masters Swimming and there were thousands of teams around the world. The age groups are five-year spans: 25-29 year-olds compete against each other, 30- to 34-year-olds, 35 to 39, and so on, all the way into the 90s. I knew none of this but I found it very intriguing. And my friend who was telling me this was competing himself, and he had not been a competitive swimmer in his youth. Masters swimming is open to anyone who wants to join, as long as he or she can get back and forth effectively in the pool.

For some reason, I found the idea of joining a team as a middle-aged man enticing. I had been having trouble for years finding motivation in the gym. The running had started to take a toll on my knees. Having a team to help keep me motivated, not to mention the idea of having actual competitions to train for, somehow brought back a certain…nostalgia. I was surprised that I was even considering it. It would take more discipline than the gym. I would have to follow a team's set training schedule (albeit a casual one in comparison to the schedule in my youth). And I had my fears: What if I wasn't good enough…again?

What if I started on the team and then quit? The fear of failure started to creep in. If I was going to do it, I wanted to make sure I did it right and stuck with it. My subconscious started coming up with reasons not to do it: It's childish to want to compete again. I used to hate swimming, why even consider it? I'm too old and it has been too long, there is no way I can start again, etc. For months I considered the pros and cons. The bottom line was I was afraid of leaving my comfort zone.

Then one night at dinner I asked my wife, son, and daughter what they thought. I explained that if I joined there would be some evenings when I would be home late because of practice, or a few weekends per year where I might be at a competition. The family agreed that I should try it: a full consensus of support (although I suspect that my teenage kids really didn't care one way or the other!). We agreed that I would, but that I would not make the same mistake I did when I was a kid. Instead of focusing on winning, I would focus on enjoying the swimming itself, the practices, the camaraderie, the physical fitness, and occasionally the fresh air. On one specific point my wife was adamant: I should join only if I was going to do it for the right reasons ...*and not for my ego.*

I looked into some teams in town and arranged to join a practice of a local team. They were happy to let me come by the pool and check it out myself. The captain of the team explained how the practices and fee structure worked and let me practice a few times with them before I decided if I wanted to join. This particular team had about 60 members ranging in age from 22 to 72, with most of the swimmers in their 30s, 40s, and 50s. They rented out lanes at a couple of pools in town four times per week and the team captain would plan the trainings. In the summer months the trainings would move outdoors. There would usually be about 10 to 15 members at any given training session.

The practices, after not having really swum for so long, were grueling for me. I could not even finish many of the sets and would frequently have to take a break to catch my breath. I had forgotten how exhausting swimming could be! Not only are you getting a full body muscle workout, but the aerobic aspect is also extreme, especially if you are not in swimming shape. It is one thing to swim back and forth in the pool at your own pace. It is entirely another to keep up with seasoned swimmers for an entire hour, alternating all four strokes with various sets in timed intervals. Practices were usually about 2,500m per one-hour session, mixing in various strokes during a workout. This amount of distance per hour is pretty standard for Masters teams. (In the appendix you will find a few Masters-level workouts.) Despite the intensity of the workout, I was hooked.

It turns out, there is adrenalin and an excitement when training with a team, even as an adult! You are motivated to keep up (or stay ahead). There is a collective satisfaction in accomplishing something as a team, even something as simple as a one-hour workout. There is poolside chatter of upcoming trainings and competitions, and a social aspect as well (team meetings usually include a couple beers). I found the entire atmosphere more motivating and supportive than I had remembered from my younger days. It was relaxed, yet focused. And the swimmers were all, without exception, happy to be there. The group respected that we all had our own reasons for being there, and only rarely is it to dominate in the pool. Instead, the real common denominator of the group is the enjoyment of the swimming itself.

I joined the team in January of 2017 and no sooner had I done so than our team captain told me we had a meet coming up. I had anticipated competing again, despite how strange that idea seemed to me as a 47 year-old. It would take me awhile to get used to fact that middle-aged people competed against each other regularly, in a highly organized fashion, with swim meets throughout the year and throughout the country, and the world. Regardless, I began training a couple times a week, and then after just a month, three times a week. I cannot emphasize enough how hard these workouts were for me compared to going to the gym or for a 5-kilometer run. It took me months to get used to the intensity during the workout, and for my body to finally stop being so sore for days after each one. If you are in a gym, you can go at your own pace, adapt the workout to your mood and to your energy level. When swimming with a team, there is pressure to go all in, to keep up with the other swimmers in your lane and to complete each set. These are not the official rules, mind you, but it is the common practice, and just about everyone abides by it. It's also what makes you faster, stronger and more disciplined. Finding the right group, and then the right lane within that group, makes an enormous difference in encouraging you to push your limits.

After a couple months of training, I headed to Bratislava for my first swim meet as an adult. It was the Slovak National Championships and run as an invitational, meaning that teams and swimmers from other countries were welcome. In this case, most of the teams were Slovak, with quite a few Czech and Polish teams making the trip, and then some individual swimmers from elsewhere in Europe. I swam the 50m, 100m and 200m free, along with the 50m fly and 50m back, and two relays. With only two months of training, my times were painfully slow compared to how I swam in my teens. I admit, I had delusional expectations about how my times should be. I have heard this can be common: youthful mindset but a middle-aged body! But even worse than that, I was exhausted after each race. Never as a young swimmer do I remember being so tired. It made sense, though: I mean, when was the last time I competed in anything at 100%? How often had I given a 100% physical effort in the last 30 years? And here I did so seven times over two days. My body could barely handle it. I returned home after the two-day event tired and sore…but exhilarated.

My point in mentioning this start of my Masters swimming career is to emphasize that it is not easy. Even as a swimmer who had spent thousands of hours in the pool, I was barely ready to get back into it. Our bodies and minds change so much as adults that getting both back in shape to compete was much harder than I thought it would be. But I loved it. I did manage to bring home a few medals, even though receiving them seemed silly to me at the time. I remember thinking, do adults really need medals? I have gotten used to it since then and have come to appreciate the medals and the occasional trophy as a genuinely nice added bonus to all the other benefits of Masters swimming.

After seeing my times and feeling my level of exhaustion at the end of the races, I decided I needed to train more. I added another day of training each week, upping it to four. The World Masters Championships were coming up that summer in Budapest and I wanted to be ready.

And it was at this point when I may have strayed from my original goal of swimming only for the right reasons, and not for victory, not to "be the best." I mean, yes, I was swimming to get in better shape, to have like-minded people around me, and to improve my times. Those were the official reasons that I told myself and others, and I believed them. Until one day my wife said my ego was taking over. I disagreed, repeating the official reasons I swam. She emphasized, in a not-so-gentle way, that my ego was indeed taking over and it would not end well. She knew my competitive spirit was starting to override my official reasoning. I either couldn't see it, or wouldn't admit it, or both, but my old programming was coming back into play, driving me to be the best. Not just the best that I could be, there is nothing wrong with that, but being *the* best: whether it be on the team, in my age group, or in a swim meet. She could hear it as a subtext in our conversations, and in my conversations with others. If I knew that this "over-competitiveness" was the reason I turned against swimming to begin with, why would I welcome it back into my life? It was ridiculous even to consider.

But it was true. Rather than having a drive to improve for healthy reasons, I was driven (albeit subconsciously) to train harder so that I could win. And when the drive comes from the wrong reasons, one makes bad decisions. I pushed a little too hard and found myself in the doctor's office. In each training I had been swimming harder and harder, trying to keep up with and then pass other swimmers my age and younger. And these are swimmers who had been Masters swimmers for years. Rather than giving my body the amount of time it needed to adapt to the new training regimen, I hurried it and did not listen when my body complained. I started to have problems sleeping and would occasionally see "stars" at random times during the day or after swim sessions. Sometimes I would wake up in the middle of the night and feel my heart beating rapidly.

The doctor measured my blood pressure over a 24-hour period and determined that I had some strange blood pressure fluctuations. No one in my family ever had such issues, so I was taken aback. He recommended taking it easy. At that point I had been training so hard that I was again perpetually tired, just like in the old days. I was so embarrassed by this that I did not even mention that part to my doctor. I didn't need to; he could see it in my test results. The bottom line was I was training too hard, and my heart could not keep up. I had to take it down a notch.

If you're swimming for the right reasons and in the proper way, there is zero chance it will send you to the doctor's office. Swimming is the healthiest of activities and has only positive benefits to offer. The fact that I was having blood pressure issues was a clear sign that I had to get my priorities in order.

Diving Back In

It was difficult. You can't simply change years of programming, especially when that programming came during your formative years. You need to work at changing it day after day, replacing your old thoughts with new ones. Specifically, I was replacing thoughts such as, "You need to beat so-and-so in the next lane," with, "Let's just have fun with this set." And changing, "I want to finally take gold next month at the swim meet," with, "During today's workout I will try to kick three underwater dolphin kicks after each turn for the entire practice." (Getting as much distance as possible with each turn is a key factor in any race, and yet practices rarely focus on the turns themselves. Trying to do three dolphin kicks - kicking both legs at the same time - each time you push off the wall in a streamlined position is a great way to practice how to gain time with each turn.) It takes real awareness to notice when those old thoughts start to seep back in. And determination to replace them day after day and knowing how best to do that.

I began to work on myself and my reasons for swimming. After slowly but successfully working on my priorities, I began to enjoy my time in the pool much more. Each practice became a time to enjoy the actual swimming, the work on the various aspects of my stroke, the satisfaction of a good workout, the feeling of the water itself, and, of course, the camaraderie. At one point, while stretching with the team on a beautiful summer day before a practice at a 50-meter outdoor pool on the south side of Prague, I realized how happy I felt. It wasn't just the weather or the group of friends or the prospect of a good practice, it was everything together. That feeling is the one that swimming can bring, and it can last a lifetime.

This idea of "being the best" that was drilled into us in my youth has its benefits, but they are short-term and do not work for everyone. If you are an elite swimmer and consistently have a chance to win a medal, this motivation can work well. But if you are one of the others who does not have a chance at the top three positions, how long can that motivate you? As I was growing up, the coaches came up with the idea of "personal best." A focus on personal bests (or, PBs, as we call them) concentrates on bettering your own times, rather than beating the swimmer next to you. This is clearly the healthier focus, can be much more inclusive in its application, and many of my coaches often discussed it and encouraged it in many of the swimmers. But the constant subtext in age-group swimming, whether from the other swimmers, parents, or the media, was to go for the gold, to bring in points for the team, and to progress to more competitive swim meets.

I got my ego under control, my priorities straight, and began to enjoy swimming for the right reasons. I decided life is too short to suffer during practices, agonize about lost swim competitions, stress about various what-ifs, and then only on occasion celebrate a victory here or there. Instead, I would focus on enjoying every aspect of what it takes to be a swimmer.

I looked forward to the practices more and began to swim the other strokes more often, even though I knew I would never compete well in any of them except freestyle. I spent more time kicking, even though it was the weakest part of my swimming (and I would invariably end up the last in my lane during every set). I spoke to other swimmers about why they are swimming and what parts of it they enjoy the most.

I didn't stress over missing a day or two because of work or family obligations. I didn't push myself overly hard, damaging myself in the process. Instead, I let my abilities develop, taking their own time, and enjoying the slow and steady improvement along the way. I ended up becoming the team coach for the last few years, designing our daily trainings so that the team got the most out of each workout.

Having a specific swim workout printed out in advance before each swim practice provides order in a team. Masters teams often do not have a coach walking alongside the pool like age-group and college teams. Instead, the coach is in the water with everybody else, swimming the same sets. Writing the workouts in advance means that the coach cannot change the sets or intervals depending on how he himself feels. I began printing our swim workouts regularly for this reason and did my best to make sure that they were challenging, but doable for the majority of the team.

And even with this more relaxed and even-keeled tempo and attitude, my race times decreased, and I managed to rack up plenty more PBs. I learned that you do not have to force it to make progress.

Thinking Outside the Pool

There are a few types of swimmers out there. Age-group swimmers are pool swimmers. Within this category there is short-course (25-meter pool) and long-course (50-meter pool). The U.S. also differentiates between yard pools and meter pools. Generally, sprinters prefer training and racing short-course, and medium and long-distance swimmers prefer long-course. The main difference is the number of flip-turns during a race or training session, giving a swimmer a small rest and a chance to get an extra push off the wall. If you are a sprinter you want that extra boost of speed from the wall more often, whereas if you are a mid or long-distance swimmer you do not want to have too many turns interrupting your much-needed rhythm. Regular breathing plays more of a role in the medium and long events, and each flip-turn forces you to hold your breath for a longer period while under the water.

Pool swimmers like the comfort of consistent pool temperatures, clear and chlorinated water, starting blocks, and the ever-present black line painted on the bottom of the pool for them to follow. Remove any one of these things and the pool swimmer will be thrown off his game. The pool is 2°C colder than it should be during a practice? Half the swimmers will be talking about it for the entire practice. Unexpected cloudiness in the water during a swim meet? Most pool swimmers will be concerned about its effect on their times and turns all weekend long. Imagine these swimmers like finely tuned race cars that need to be on the proper track, at the right temperature, and with the right humidity.

Outdoor swimmers, on the other hand, have none of the above, and instead rely on an entirely different set of conditions. They are more like rally race cars, ready to tear it up, no matter the conditions. Outdoor swimming occurs in lakes, rivers and canals, even in the open sea itself. Triathletes train in outdoor swimming for the swimming leg of triathlons. To swim in competitive outdoor events, you need additional skills. Yes, basically being a good swimmer is the core strength, but other abilities come into play. You need to know how to start a race while in a large group, often with hundreds of other swimmers. You need to know how to "spot", meaning how to swim in a straight line (there is no line on the bottom of the lake!). This skill is surprisingly more difficult than it sounds. How to turn around a buoy efficiently. How to breathe more carefully without swallowing any water. The consequences of swallowing dirty lake water can be much worse than swallowing chlorinated water. How to withstand cooler temperatures or learn to swim with a wet suit. And then, most importantly, you need to know how to pace yourself, because the longest races in all of swimming are the outdoor races. Usually outdoor races start at 1km, building to 3km, 5km and 10km races (the 10km is equivalent to running a marathon). The longest race, the ultra-marathon of swimming, is the 20km race.

Surprisingly, there are not many swimmers who swim both pool competitions as well as outdoor. In general, there are more outdoor swimmers, and the competitions tend to draw larger crowds. Neither sport is ideal for spectators, but the outdoor events have the added draw of being, well, outdoors. The conditions on a beautiful day are entirely more enjoyable than even the best day inside at a sauna-like indoor swim meet. My parents and brother can explain in detail about the countless weekends they endured sitting in the humid, chlorine-saturated air at swim meets, waiting for hours in between each of my events. Outside, you have the added advantage of beaches, food and drink stands, and other attractive activities rather than just sitting in the stands waiting for long periods for your friend's or loved one's event to come up.

The last category of swimming is cold-water swimming, or ice swimming. This group of unusual individuals likes to combine cold-water exposure and competitive swimming. Often these competitions, mostly held in lakes and rivers during the winter months, take place in water from 1 to 5 degrees Celsius (32-41°F). For this type of event, the core ability is handling the cold for longer times, rather than swimming fast. A mediocre swimmer who is well-acclimated to the cold will often beat a fast swimmer who is newer to cold temperatures. Distances usually start at 250m and go up to a kilometer. Under normal circumstances I would not have considered this an option for me. The cold water can be extremely painful: to get an idea, put a bunch of ice cubes in a bowl of water and stick your hand in. See how long you can keep it in. Most people last only a few seconds, and that is only your hand! Imagine putting your entire body in and then trying to swim for up to 20 minutes.

During the first Covid lockdown in March of 2020, the Czech government closed all pools in the country. A few weeks went by and my distance swimmer friend called to say she and another couple of our friends had been training in a nearby lake. By that time it was April and the weather was warming up. But the lake temperatures were still only 12 to 14 degrees Celsius (53-57°F). I said I did not have a wetsuit, and she explained that neither did she or the other two people she was swimming with. So, I headed out to the lake. It was nearby and just a 20-minute bike ride away. I rode up, we all suited up, and we got in the water. I was so shocked and surprised by how cold the water was that I would not have continued, except that my friends went in and just started swimming. If they can do it, so can I, I thought, and I swam after them. But they kept going, swimming the entire kilometer length before turning around to swim back. I thought it best to turn around after just a few hundred meters and got out after about five minutes. At that point, I still was not sure how my body was going to handle the cold and I did not want to push it too far. Acclimating to the cold water can take months, and I wanted to feel how much I could handle step by step.

    Once I got out and dried off, I was fine. I was not shivering, a good sign. Shivering after you get out of the cold can be normal, as your body tries to return to its core temperature. The only real concern is if you start shivering while you are still in the water. If that happens, you are to get out immediately, dry off, put on warm clothes, and have a warm drink. That day I may have not gotten a workout in, but I discovered something even more important: I liked swimming in the wild…and in the cold. It reminded me of those fun times as a kid, jumping in the lake, feeling the weightlessness, the shock of the cold and being able to handle it. The great memories came back and it was fun. And it was exhilarating! After a cold-water swim, you have an energy boost for the rest of the day, as well as an elevated mood. I began training regularly with this group. We swam in that lake, in the river, and in other lakes. I slowly increased my distances until I was able to swim with them the entire time. I think our total cold exposure at that point never went past about 30 or 40 minutes. Once the pools reopened though, we stopped most of the outdoor swimming. We returned to the comfort of the pool, where we could swim longer and more varied workouts.

Thanks to toning down my ego and swimming for swimming's sake, and for the multitude of other benefits, I began to think of competing outside of the pool. I had a friend on our swim team who, although she rarely spoke of it, I noticed swam regularly in outdoor events. I asked her about them and if she recommended them. Her eyes lit up with surprise. No one else on our 60-person team had ever even asked. She explained how to sign up and sent me a link to upcoming races. Even though at that point I had not swum once in an outdoor event, and even though the longest race I had ever swum as an adult was 400m, I signed up. I was ready to see what new challenges could bring. If I had been interested only in winning, I would not have signed up. It had nothing to do with winning or being the best. Instead, I wanted to see what else swimming had to offer me: what was out there if I got out of my comfort zone yet again?

My first race was a 1km race in the south of the Czech Republic. I signed up and was nervous as hell. This time I was not nervous about taking gold or getting a best time, I was nervous about just finishing and not totally exhausting myself. I wanted to set my pace and stick with it. Swimming 1km is an entirely different race than a 200m or 400m, and I was not confident about my ability to not only know, but also to stick with, my pace while the adrenalin was pulsing through my veins. What made it easier was that my friend was swimming the 5km. So how hard could my race be if it was only 1km? I swam it, I managed my speed, and I loved it. I had issues with spotting, though, and often veered to the right instead of swimming in a straight line. I probably added another 200m of swimming because of this. And I swallowed water while trying to figure out how to spot and breathe at the same time - another skill that most pool swimmers do not have. But, despite these hang-ups, I was hooked on this new type of competition. The thrill of running into the water with hundreds of other swimmers, the adrenalin of having to fight for your position through a multitude of kicking legs and swinging arms: It was an entirely different experience than climbing onto a block and diving at the "beep." And then there's the race itself: After you get into a rhythm and the swimmers disperse, each according to his or her own speed, you find yourself in the middle of the lake, on a beautiful day, doing something that you love, and are in a competition on top of that, pushing your body's limits, feeling how it adapts to the temperature and to the other conditions. It's awesome. And it's addicting. With outdoor swimming it is much more about the environment, the feeling, the thrill of the race itself, than it is about winning.

Swimming for the right reasons opened outdoor swimming to me, and I began to swim in outdoor river and lake races from 600m to 3km. I will continue with these and hope to be able to swim a 10km race one day soon. The only way to be able to even consider a race like the 10k is to enjoy the process. If you think of each practice as a grueling chore, you will not want to have to do the number of practices necessary to swim a 10km race. But if each practice is viewed as a reward, as desirable in and of itself, then even a long race is just something than would fall naturally into place.

Beyond the Race

Once you learn to love swimming for the right reasons, you start consciously and subconsciously looking for extra reasons and places to swim. You measure possible vacation destinations in a different way: Does the hotel have a pool? Is the sea calm enough for swimming? Do the jellyfish sting? Will I get to see some turtles? And then you find yourself swimming along the beaches, across lakes, around in circles in the bay, even in water that is far too cold for the less dedicated swimmer. And each time after taking the plunge and getting in your 500m or 5km, the rest of your day has just improved. You not only have the feeling of having exercised, but of having conquered a new challenge, either mental or physical or both. You have seized the day. And the feeling of well-being that comes with that can be addictive. And that is the true victory: It's better than any medal, and it's entirely within your own control.

You don't need to go to the Olympics to get the most out of swimming. In fact, if you work on it as an adult, you can get more out of swimming than most Olympians. By the time they finish their careers, many top swimmers do not want to put on their goggles ever again. For the rest of us, it can be the opposite: The end of swimming for us as youths can be a new beginning for a deeply pleasurable and healthy lifetime of swimming.

The following pages contain my tips on getting the most out of the various types of swimming. I try not to get too technical and instead focus on the various options to excel in each category. There are a few break-out boxes that go into some detail. These should be skipped unless you are geeky concerning your gear.

In the appendix, there are trainings for outdoor and indoor workouts, along with a list of recommended books.

Getting Started
or Restarted

The gear:

The essentials you need for swimming are pretty simple: goggles and a swimsuit. If you have long hair and swim in a pool, then most pools require a swim cap as well. That is really all you need for your entire swimming career. There are plenty of things you can add as you go, as your workouts become more specific, such as fins, kickboards, pull-buoys, hand-paddles, etc., but they are not essential. I will recommend other books that go into detail on the pros and cons of the other swimming aids. For the purposes of this book, we will focus on the basics.

The Lowdown on Goggles

Choosing goggles should not be difficult. There are two requirements: They must not leak, and they must be comfortable. With goggles that have these two qualities, you can swim. If your goggles are not both, it is time to get new ones. Ask around to see what brands and styles your friends or other swimmers prefer.

There are other details to consider once you decide to swim regularly and in various environments. Clear goggles are OK for indoor pools but are hard on the eyes if you are swimming outside on a sunny day. For outdoor swimming I recommend getting goggles with dark blue, or brown, or even mirrored lenses.

If you wear glasses or contacts, you can find prescription goggles from reputable brands at your local swim store and online. For these, I recommend buying them off the shelf with the closest prescription to your own, rather than ordering goggles with your exact prescription. The cost difference is usually not worth it, and in the pool you need to see well, not perfectly.

Make sure to never touch the inside of the goggles with your fingers. The lenses have an anti-fog coating that can be wiped off with an aggressive finger. Instead, only rinse your goggles with water. And if you have issues with them fogging up, use soapy water and let the goggles air dry.

The Commitment

The great Yogi Berra has been quoted many times as saying, "Half the game is 90 percent mental." Yes, humorous, but also illustrative of how important our "mental game" is. In this case, the mental game is our approach to swimming: our attitude toward the trainings, our focus on putting our time in the water high on our priority list. There are many tricks and systems on how to get yourself to regularly do something until it becomes a habit. Hopefully, you know what works for you, whether it's just adding it to your schedule, paying in advance for lessons or pool time, joining a team, engaging a swim coach, or punishing or rewarding yourself for each practice completed or not completed. All of the above can work for people, and choosing what works best for you is important. Be realistic. Don't schedule swimming five times a week if you are a busy person and the pool is an hour away. Start with fewer trainings but be sure to keep them regular. This will help you to form the habit. And it's once swimming becomes a habit that the magic happens.

Classic habit blockers can intercede, so be prepared. Our subconscious, until we program it otherwise, can work overtime to stop us from getting out of our comfort zone. We need to be ready for this and take precautions. We know why we want to swim, but our subconscious can come up with tens of reasons not to swim: You have work to do, you are too tired, you didn't get enough sleep, you can swim tomorrow, you can run instead, you deserve a day off, it's too beautiful a day to go indoors to swim, it's raining too hard, you are still sore from yesterday. You get the idea. There will always be a mental battle, and you need to prepare for it to win it. That means breaking down as many barriers to your goal as possible in advance.

Make getting to the pool as easy as possible. Have your swimsuit and gear in your bag and ready to go. Make sure your car has enough gas. Know the exact route you will take to get to the pool and how much traffic you can anticipate. Schedule your time so that you can finish your essential obligations either before or after. Turn off your phone if you know a distracting call might come in. Most importantly, know yourself and your own tendencies and plan accordingly. Although these tactics are more important at the beginning as you develop these healthy new habits, they could easily continue in one way or another for

Diving Back In

years. I have found it helpful to replace each excuse not to swim with an excuse *to* swim. Just as your brain can trick you into not doing something, you can trick yourself into doing it. You can replace those excuses not to swim with your reasons *to* swim: I will feel great once I get in, I will just dive in and see how I feel, I will go tonight but sleep in tomorrow, I will go and just take it easy, etc. Anything you need to tell yourself to get to the pool and jump in. Once you're in, the barriers and excuses fade away.

This may sound strange, but also make sure that you have a swimsuit you feel comfortable in. Swimmers spend a lot of time getting in and out of suits and over time have become comfortable with their bodies. But if you are new to swimming, or are getting back after a long break, it can take some getting used to the fact that you are basically half naked most of the time at the pool. Feeling comfortable in your own skin, and then also in your swimsuit, is key to wanting to go to the pool. In fact, one of the main reasons that there are not more people swimming regularly is because many do not want to spend too much time in public in their swimsuit. If this is your situation, my suggestion is to find a swimsuit you like, know that no one is judging you, go to the pool, and swim like no one is watching – because no one is!

Diving In

After you have your suit and have scheduled some pool time; just get in and swim. Find a lane in a pool that is designated for lap swimming and get in and swim your laps. I do not recommend trying to swim in a pool that does not have a specific area for lap swimming. Unless you are the only one in such a pool, it is just too dangerous for everyone. Give yourself an amount of time that you want to spend in the pool- generally from 30 minutes to an hour- and get in there and just swim. If you prefer breaststroke, swim breast. If freestyle, then free. If all four strokes, then mix it up. If you feel winded and need a break, pause at the wall and give yourself a few breaths. Then get back out there. Do this a few times, maybe every other day or so, counting your laps and meters, and writing down after each practice how much time you swam and how far you went. Recording your progress is for you only and can help as you plan future workouts.

On Stretching

Stretching out before and after you swim will help you over the long term. You need flexibility to swim well. A flexible upper body will enable you to take longer and stronger strokes. Foot and leg flexibility will help you kick more efficiently. Despite this, many swimmers skip stretching both before and after workouts. I must admit I am also often guilty of this. You can stretch out while swimming your warm-up in the pool, and after a workout many people are in a hurry to head home so decide to skip that stretching too. If you want to get the most out of your training session, and be less sore afterwards, then be sure to stretch both times. But if you are really pressed for time, I wouldn't sweat missing a stretching session or two, especially if you can make up for it after you get back home.

Choosing the Pool

Make sure that you like the pool and the facilities. If the locker rooms are lousy, if the pool is cloudy, or if it's just too often too full of swimmers, you might want to look for other options. After all, there are enough barriers out there to stop you from developing your new habit, so you don't want to add yet another one to the list. Instead, check out online forums, or make some calls to other pools, and ask around for what seems more your style. Also find out which times you can swim, and which of those times are the least crowded. Generally, the fewer people with you in the lane, the better.

Pool Etiquette

There can be slow swimmers blocking your path, and faster swimmers cruising past you. This is all part of swimming in public pools, so don't get discouraged. Instead, make sure you are in the lane that has the most swimmers going the closest to your speed and stick with it. If you need to pass someone, gently touch their feet and start to swim around them, staying in the middle of the lane to avoid oncoming traffic. If someone taps your foot, or starts to pass you, move closer to the lane line to give them extra room, or even stop to let them pass. This is basic pool etiquette, and most swimmers follow it. Until they don't. Every pool has the oblivious swimmer who doesn't know how fast he is going, what lane he is in, or even what stroke he is swimming. Try and avoid these clueless swimmers. They are dangerous to us all, annoying, and the best option is to change lanes.

After developing or redeveloping the healthy habit of swimming regularly, you can slowly turn it up a notch. If you are happy with 500m of breaststroke over a 30-minute period, then that is great, and you might want to stop reading here. A lot of the satisfaction from swimming comes from pushing your limits, challenging your body, and fine-tuning your technique. If you have any health conditions that require you not to push yourself, then follow your doctor's advice first and foremost. If not, then start slowly raising the level of intensity. Adding time and distance are the most obvious options. You might want to add 100m to each workout for 10 workouts. You might want to build from 1km to 3km per session. Or, if 2km currently takes you an hour, you might want to shorten your time, bit by bit, over a month. Write down your results. As you see yourself shortening your times, or extending your distances, you will not only feel great, but you will also enjoy each session, each improvement, more and more.

Once you are back in the habit and have increased your distances and speed, you should start planning more varied workouts. A planned workout, for example, could consist of a warm-up, a build set, a main set, a drill set, and a cool-down set. Warm-ups can be from 200 to 1,000m. Build sets start to slowly increase your speed and often include other strokes besides freestyle and can be from 200m to 500m. Main sets usually are from 500m to 1,500m depending on your ability.

A drill set usually is from 200m to 500m and a cool-down is usually around 200m. A simple workout could be the following:

Warm-up: 400m easy freestyle

Build: 3 x 100 individual medley (25m butterfly, 25m backstroke, 25m breaststroke, and 25m freestyle) with 30 seconds in between each one. (If you can't swim butterfly yet, you can substitute another stroke or work on a one-armed butterfly until you are able to get both arms working well together.)

Main: 5 x 100m free on 2-minute intervals

Drill set: 3 x 100m free, focusing on long strokes, keeping your elbows high, and dragging your fingertips next to your body on the recovery (recovery is when your arm has finished its pull, has exited the water next to your waist, and needs to "recover" back to its entry point)

Cool-down: 200m very easy and slow

Total: 1,700m

Diving Back In

With time you will develop the elusive "feel for the water." Swimmers refer to having - or losing - their "feel for the water" quite often. They are referring to their efficiency. If you can be efficient in the water, you can swim longer and faster. Imagine an Olympic swimmer's freestyle compared to the freestyle of the average Joe: The Olympian gets more distance and speed per stroke while expending less energy. To do this, you need to feel the water itself with each stroke. You need to feel where you are expending energy without gaining maximum propulsion. It is about learning to feel the difference when you are grabbing moving water (not ideal) and when you are grabbing nonmoving water (ideal). You will also feel if you are pushing yourself through the water like a barge or gliding through the water like a sailboat. Working on your "feel for the water," on improving your efficiency, is what forms the key to any healthy swimming addiction. It is a lifelong pursuit. As you make progress and discoveries in each session, be sure to write these down too in your workout journal. If you learn something good today, you want to remember it tomorrow.

There is enough satisfaction and pleasure to gain from regular solo swim sessions to keep many people swimming regularly for the rest of their lives. Many do not want to head to the office until they have put their laps in. Many look forward to the lunch break for a swim session that gives them an energy boost for the rest of the day. Many people not only feel great during and after this type of swimming, but also see significant results in their physique. If this is enough for you, great. Working on your efficiency in the comfort of a heated and chlorinated pool, increasing your distances and speeds, building to a more varied format, is so rewarding in and of itself, that it is plenty for a lifetime of swimming enjoyment.

Swimming with friends is another way to add to your experience. Friends can help to keep you motivated, can often teach you new things in the pool, and add a social element to your regular workouts. I am a very social person, so swimming with others is a huge motivator for me. But there are also times when I just want to get into the water, swim the laps and work on my strokes - primarily freestyle, my turns, or my underwaters (the time from when you push off the wall until you surface), without having to worry about being social or following a prescribed workout. On these occasions (for me about once a week), swimming is like an active meditation, taking my mind off all the other concerns I have to deal with outside of the pool, and instead concentrating only on each stroke, each turn, each breath. When conditions are right, you can achieve a mindfulness in the buoyancy of the water and the easy rhythm of your stroke. This is difficult when swimming with others.

Diving Back In

If you want to take it to the next level, there are the options I mentioned before. Only you can decide if Masters swimming or outdoor swimming is more appropriate to you. Many people think that becoming a Masters swimmer means that they have to swim in competitions. There are many Masters competitions throughout the year, but believe it or not, most Masters swimmers do not compete. The majority join Masters swim teams for other reasons, the most popular being physical fitness. Teams usually have a coach who plans the various workouts. They have rented lanes, and group people together according to ability. And teams bring like-minded people together who generally tend to encourage one another to continue to build and enjoy their swimming abilities. If this option seems attractive to you, you can find local teams to choose from online or on social media.

The outdoor swimming option is a bit more adventurous. Here the teams are more focused on competitions, either swimming or triathlons, rather than fitness. This does not mean all outdoor swimmers are top athletes; that is far from the case. You have swimmers of all abilities on these teams, and if you can train with the team, you will be welcome no matter what your level. Outdoor teams train in pools as well as lakes and rivers. Depending on the climate, many swimmers train regularly in wet suits. And most importantly, they like swimming in just about any kind of water. If you need to see through the water to want to swim in it, outdoor swimming is *clearly* not for you. Outdoor swimmers are in it for the adventure and for continuous challenges beyond just time, distance, and speed. When you see people in your local lake or river swimming in the rain when it is 12°C outside? Yes, those are the outdoor types. Although I never thought this swimming was for me, the more I swim outdoors "in the wild" the more I enjoy it. There is a thrill, a different kind of rush, as you swim across a lake or in a river with the ducks and swans. I even swim with a group on occasion that, because of work schedules, often must train in the river in the evening when it's dark! Certainly, this option is not for the timid, and not necessarily recommended, but the camaraderie after even just a single workout session outside can be invigorating!

If you do opt to try this out, there is one more piece of essential gear that you will need: a swim buoy. These buoys are like thick balloons made from PVC with a cord that you fasten around your waist. They usually come in neon colors so that they are easily visible from far away. There are often pockets in them where you can fit a flashlight for night swimming, or your car keys or money in case there is no safe place for them on land. In no way do these buoys help you swim. Instead, they increase your visibility to keep you safe from boats, kayaks, paddle boarders, etc. Most also have the extra benefit of being able to hold you up in the water if you want or need to take a break. Another word of caution before you train outdoors: try and always swim with someone else, preferably an experienced swimmer, or better yet a group.

Safety first, after all, so also make sure that the area where you want to swim is safe. If in a river, make sure you know the speed of the current. If it's a lake, make sure that the water is not polluted. Check the temperature, and if it's cold, make sure that you know how long you are able to stay in the water. Map the area you plan to swim and get an idea of the distances from landmark to landmark. And check the entry and exit points, making sure you can get in and out easily and without cutting your feet on broken glass or sharp rocks. I realize it sounds like a lot of factors, but in the end the adventure can be well worth the small amount of time and preparation needed to scout out your next swim.

In addition to all the benefits I already mentioned, there are others as well. Swimming can be amazing for you. Since the health benefits are generally well-known, I will not go into detail here, but the bottom line is that swimming could be the healthiest of all activities. It helps your cardiovascular system, keeps all the major muscle groups strong, builds healthy lungs, and is easy on your joints and ligaments. Regular swimming also helps to keep your weight nearer to an ideal level. My waist size went down by 2 inches during my first year as a Master swimmer and I wasn't trying to do that. It was simply a byproduct of this great new activity. And swimming is not a sport you will need to give up at a certain age. Instead, it could easily happen that you enjoy swimming more and more as the years go by. At the Masters swim meets, the loudest roars of applause are when a 90+-year-old swimmer finishes his or her race.

******

I wrote this book to share my love of swimming and in the hopes of helping anyone who has ever considered swimming, to start. Or to help anyone who had ceased swimming, as I had, to get back in the water. There is so much reward and satisfaction, so much exhilaration and fun, to be found by simply putting on a swimsuit and goggles and diving in. I had forgotten this as a teenager, and it took years before I was ready to come back to it. But now that I have, I am enjoying it more than ever.

I hope you have found something here that might bring you to the pool. For me, it was a surprise at lunch with a friend that reopened the realm of swimming. For you, I hope

Diving Back In

it will be reading this story. If you have enjoyed this book, please check out my list of recommended reading below. And swim on! ☺

Appendix A

Swim Workout Examples

The beginning. After you are ready and able to go beyond swimming a few laps at your own pace, this is a good workout to get you started on a more varied program:

Warm-up: 300m choice of strokes

Build session: 4 x 50m freestyle where you swim the first 25m fast, and the second 25m easy. Take 30 seconds rest in between 50s

Main set: 4 x 100m: 100m free, 100m choice, 100m free, 100m choice

Diving Back In

Take 30 seconds between each 100.

After the set, swim an easy 50m

Kick set: 4 x 50m kicking any style you want with 15 seconds in between

Cool-down: 150m easy

Total distance: 1,300m

Intermediate When you are ready to turn it up a notch, here is a medium-level workout (that includes some butterfly):

Warm-up: 400m choice

Build: 2 x 100m individual medleys with 30 seconds in between

Main: 10 x 50m free on 60 seconds (or 1:10, whatever interval gives you about 20 seconds rest after the first 50m), Swim 50m easy after this set.

Main II: 3 x 100m choice but not free, with 20 seconds after each one

Drill set: 4 x 50m easy freestyle, focusing (as I mentioned earlier) on dragging your fingertips next to your body during the recovery

Cool-down: 200m choice, easy

Total distance: 1,850 meters

Here is an example of a Masters-level workout:

Diving Back In

Warm-up: 600m choice

Build session: 6 x 50m the first five strokes butterfly, then finish each 50 with easy freestyle

Main: 4 x 100m individual medley with 20 seconds in between each

Main II: 6 x 100m freestyle on a 1:30 interval (or 1:40)

100m easy after this set

Drill set: 4 x 100m of the stroke and drill of your choice, with fins, with 20 seconds in between each

4 x 50m: 25m underwater with a 25m sprint of the stroke of your choice

30 seconds rest after each 50

200m cool-down

Total distance: 2,800 meters

Appendix B

Recommended Reading

Atomic Habits: An Easy and Proven Way to Build Good Habits and Break Bad Ones, by James Clear, Cornerstone Digital; 1st edition (October 18, 2018). If you have trouble developing new and healthy habits in your life, then this book is a must-read.

Swim Smooth: The Complete Coaching System for Swimmers and Triathletes, by Paul Newsome and Adam Young, Fernhurst Books Limited; 2nd edition (June 15, 2012). This is a go-to reference book for swimmers of all levels and has in-depth information on swimming styles and types, not to mention detailed breakdowns of all the various items of swimming equipment along with their pros and cons.

Total Immersion: The Revolutionary Way To Swim Better, Faster, and Easier, by Terry Laughlin, Touchstone, (March 13, 2012). If you did not learn how to swim well while you were young, it used to be thought that you had missed the boat and that you would never be able to swim as an adult as well as those who started as kids. This book changed all that and revolutionized the way adults learn how to swim.

The Wim Hof Method: Activate Your Full Human Potential, by Wim Hof and Elissa Epel PhD, Sounds True (October 20, 2020). If you are interested in swimming in cold water, Wim is the guru. This book also instructs you on his three-pillar method for improving your health, happiness, and strength: Breathing, mental preparedness (commitment), and cold exposure.

No Limits: The Will to Succeed, by Michael Phelps, Free Press (December 9, 2008), Simply a great read from the GOAT.

Age Is Just a Number: Achieve Your Dreams at Any Stage in Your Life, by Dara Torres and Elizabeth Weil, Crown (April 7, 2009). Who can inspire us more than the oldest woman to ever medal in swimming in the Olympics?

I loved the water from day one, 1972, Vermont

Beginning to swim competitively again was exhausting, Rainbow Masters, Prague, 2018

With my teammates from our relay at the European Masters Championships in 2018, Bled, Slovenia

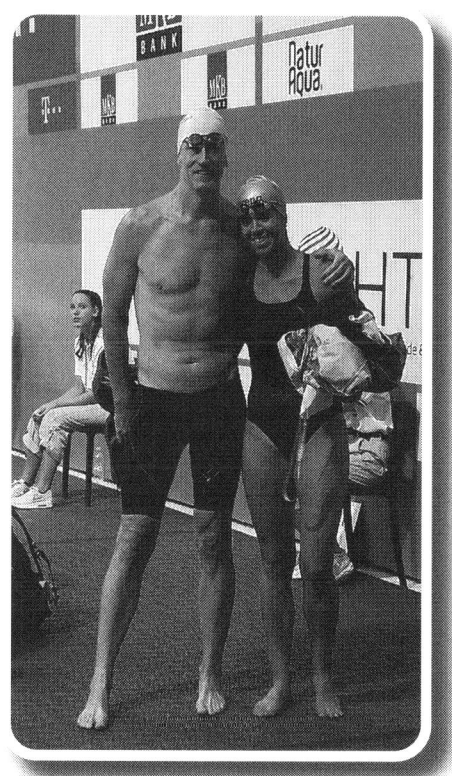

With fellow Neptun Masters teammates in Budapest
at the World Masters Championships in 2017

Even diving off the blocks was more difficult than I had remembered, Dresden 2018

The support and camaraderie from a team is irreplaceable, Jihlava, Czech Republic, 2019

Masters teams, encourage you to swim even your weaker strokes, Usti nad Labem, Czech Republic, 2019

Medals and trophies can be a nice added bonus, Czech Masters Championships, Česká Lípa, Czech Republic, 2019

Finishing my first outdoor race opened up a new world of swimming for me, 1km, Veselí nad Lužnicí, Czech Republic, 2018

Learning how to swim in a wet suit is not easy, Prague City Swim, CZ, 2019

The outdoor races draw more people and have a better atmosphere, 3km, East Bohemia, CZ

The exhilaration after each outdoor race is awesome, Veselí and Lužnicí, CZ, 2019

Swimming in Lake Michigan in October can surprise some onlookers, Chicago, IL, 2020

Swimming in my favorite spot in the world, Vermont, 2020

Swim meets can take you to cool locations that even the family might like, Budapest, 2017

Some vacation spots have ideal swimming conditions. And turtles.
Magens Bay Beach, St. Thomas

Printed in Great Britain
by Amazon